Glynn Christian's Book of . . .
Table Manners

BBC-TV chef–traveller Glynn Christian has entertained on British television since 1982. As well as over 1000 live appearances, he's made series in the Eastern Mediterranean, New Zealand, Sri Lanka, California, China, Thailand and Australia. His lively, sometimes challenging, observations combined with practical fact-sharing have established him as an unchallenged authority on gourmet and delicatessen ingredients – and how to use them. Glynn's many books include *Fragile Paradise*, the only biography of his ancestor Fletcher Christian, leader of the mutiny on *Bounty* in 1789. After 10 years in Australia and New Zealand, Glynn has recently returned to live and work in London.

Glynn Christian's Book of . . . Table Manners

For high-flyers who don't want bad behaviour to land them in the soup

With illustrations by
Donovan Bixley

NEW
HOLLAND

First published in 2005 by New Holland Publishers (NZ) Ltd
Auckland • Sydney • London • Cape Town

www.newhollandpublishers.co.nz

218 Lake Road, Northcote, Auckland, New Zealand
14 Aquatic Drive, Frenchs Forest, NSW 2086, Australia
86–88 Edgware Road, London W2 2EA, United Kingdom
80 McKenzie Street, Cape Town 8001, South Africa

ISBN: 1 86966 100 1

Managing editor: Matt Turner
Editor: Renée Lang
Design: Nick Turzynski, redinc.
Cover image: Corbis/TRANZ

A catalogue record for this book is available from the National Library of New Zealand

10 9 8 7 6 5 4 3 2 1

Colour reproduction by Pica Digital Pte Ltd, Singapore
Printed by Times Offset (M) Sdn Bhd, Malaysia

Contents

Introduction

'It is only shallow people who do not judge by appearances,' Oscar Wilde once famously said. He also said the only people who speak disrespectfully of Society are those not able to get into it. It's the same at table.

The only people who ridicule good table manners are those who have none.

Table manners count and, like it or not, you will be judged by yours.

I n the days before there were forks, when you ate with a knife, spoon and your hands from a slab of bread called a trencher, saucers were exactly what they seemed – a small, shallow dish in which sauces were served.

It didn't matter so much if you got messier fingers when you dipped food into these saucers, even if it meant your fingers would invariably dirty the salt when you reached for that. But if you crooked your little finger out of the way, this kept it clean for dipping into the pristine whiteness of the salt cellar. Very good manners for the time.

Centuries later, those wishing to seem better bred than they were continued the practice of extending a little finger, especially when drinking tea. This is the most grisly example of 'backstairs refained'; it is self-consciously precious, yet thought to be genteel by those who are mannered rather than well mannered.

'Backstairs refained' is an expression coined in Tiffany's *Book of Table Manners for Teenagers*, originally published in 1961 and recently republished. Little has changed, least of all the need for such a book, and not just for teenagers. With more and more business being done these days in cafés and restaurants, the quality of your table manners can be the difference between corporate failure and success. This will affect your social aspirations too, no matter how modest.

With more and more business being done these days in cafés and restaurants, the quality of your table manners can be the difference between corporate failure and success.

Advice on etiquette and table manners was being published six centuries ago, for those privileged few who ate at a table. Much of what was said at that time is just as pertinent today.

Ladies and gentlemen were urged to show their breeding by washing their hands before coming to table, not least because they used their hands to eat. They were told to bring only clean knives and spoons to the table, not to speak with a full mouth, and to keep their lips wiped clean. Care had to be taken not to seem gross by putting too much onto your trencher (bread) at once, not to spill sauces or food onto clothes, and not to put too much food onto your spoon and thus into your mouth. So, no changes there, then.

Breaking wind from either end was considered coarse, as was picking your teeth with your knife.

An important past exhortation was not to scratch at your skin directly, but instead to use your napkin or a corner of your clothing. If that itch were caused by a louse and you then squashed it, the cloth would absorb the blood and mess and not leave a smeared corpse on your skin.

You were obliged not to scratch your 'privities' while at table and not to put your hands on those of others, nor on the breasts of women who might be dining beside you. Breaking wind from either end was considered coarse, as was picking your teeth with your knife.

One of the worst things you could do was to eat your trencher – which by the end of a meal was fair sodden with sauces and gravies – because it was traditional to give trenchers to the poor. There is the faintest echo of this in the still-common belief it is rude to eat everything on your plate, sometimes justified as a sign the generosity of fare has been altogether too much for you. This is misplaced nicety, *naicety* even; it's the sort of thing that marks you as too feeble to know the difference between manners and pretence.

Better to eat up and think of the starving children in Italy or Africa, as every Baby Boomer child with a father who had fought in the Second World War was made to do. We also learned the futility of retorting that the starving children were indeed welcome to what sat congealing in front of us.

●

table

14

manners

Putting in the Knife

Few things are more chilling at table than hearing a person ask: 'Have you written to Mother?' It's a sneering signal to others that someone is holding their knife like a pen. It'd better not be you. And it's no good saying it's worse manners to point it out; be grateful they didn't point their finger at you and laugh outright.

Holding your knife the wrong way can lose you a job and keep you low on the corporate ladder, and nothing is more certain to keep you down on the social scale. You might feel secure amongst your own group, but venture out, go into town, or try to fly high in Europe without learning how to hold your knife and you'll stab yourself in the back every time.

The accepted rule is that the handle of your knife should be in the palm of your hand, not sticking up between your thumb and forefinger. You might well think it looks more elegant this way, but most people who count in this world think it's just plain ill-bred. It's a big problem if the person who counts is the one you'd like to marry you. They probably won't. Holding a knife the wrong way is probably worse than saying 'toilet' instead of 'lavatory' or 'loo'.

table

16

manners

Nor should you hold your knife so your fingers are so far down the blade they half cover it, for then you look like an infant promoted to the big table a year too soon. The handle is for your hand, and your forefinger rests only on the top edge. No other part of the knife should ever show a finger- or thumbprint.

The most vexed question of all is how to know which knife to use at a formal setting. Unless you are in a château in France, where cutlery can be set according to its size, you should start on the outside and work inwards. If you have bolted and started before everyone else, and then discover you are using the wrong knife, you will not be asked to leave the table.

Holding your knife the wrong way can lose you a job and keep you low on the corporate ladder, and nothing is more certain to keep you down on the social scale.

There are two correct ways to proceed. You can continue with insouciance, and when the course is finished simply hold the knife back until its turn comes around again. Or you can change as soon as you notice your gaffe, but you must do this without drawing attention to yourself, and particularly without saying something that may appear to you as endearingly self-effacing, such as 'Oh silly me! You can't take me anywhere!' There will be plenty who might agree, and so won't. Polite people will pretend not to notice and mention it only behind your back.

Sometimes, you may find an outermost extra knife on the right side of your setting. This is unkind. Sometimes it'll be a host or hostess wanting to show you how many matching cutlery pieces they have. Or it could be done deliberately to trip you up. Or it could be plain dumb. What you must do is look to your left to see if a side plate has been set. If it has, then the extra knife is your bread-and-butter knife and it should be quickly picked up and set onto that plate.

table
18
manners

If this is anything like a formal dinner, you will have the last laugh, knowing bread should never be served at dinner because the food is supposed to be generous and filling enough. Of course, if it's an informal meal, it doesn't matter; and if you are eating off your knees, dinner might be just bread anyway, sometimes disguised with a scrape of tomato and called pizza.

Steak knives and fish knives are a modern affectation and totally unnecessary; steak should be tender enough to cut with an ordinary table knife, while – in a restaurant, anyway – fish should be off the bone. There is nothing a fish knife and fork can do that ordinary cutlery cannot do as well. Fish knives at home are precious, often used only because they have been in the family for a while. The suggestion that a fish knife may be held like a pen because 'you use less pressure on fish' was only ever used by nineteenth-century cutlery manufacturers to sell the damned things.

There is nothing a fish knife
and fork can do that ordinary cutlery
cannot do as well.

If you are not given a steak knife, or a fish knife and matching fork, don't ask for them; and if you are given them, do not snort derisively. Few things are more enjoyable than quietly knowing better.

And here is the most important absolute of all. Do not eat off your knife. Ever. I have the names of three young executives, each of whom lost major promotion because they ate off their knives in a restaurant where their futures were being discussed. The delicious part is that I know why they didn't get their promotions, but they have not been told.

Could this explain why you are still doing the filing, my dear?

●

Forking
Stupid

These days it's just as likely to be your fork that keeps you no better than you should be. If you have a knife in one hand, it is wrong to have a fork in the other with the tines pointed up. It's considered by those who know best as vulgar, largely because it is usually done self-consciously, in the belief it is elegant or 'Continental'. Sleek young women in television soaps and some American film stars do it, thinking, I presume, it's elegant because it's different, or that because it's different it must be elegant. Whoah; that's the clue right there. Different? Anything different about the way you eat is almost certainly a flashy bit of 'backstairs refained'.

Anyone in the know knows the way it's been done for the past few centuries is the right way to do it.

So — you hold your knife with the handle in your palm and your fork in the other hand with the tines pointing down. Always. If you put your knife down, you can turn your fork over. It's correct to change hands when you do this, too, so if you're right-handed you would switch and eat with the fork in your right hand.

If it is your sole eating instrument, the fork should be held with the handle between the index finger and the thumb and resting on the side of your middle finger.

If you hold a fork (or spoon) with the top of the handle hidden, with your thumb and all four fingers wrapped around it, you will look like at worst an ape or at best an infant. You choose which is worse. The last person I saw eating like this was an accountant.

Of course, to eat only with a fork, your food must be bite-sized. The norm is to cut up just a small amount of food with your knife and fork. Then put down the knife, switch hands with the fork and eat using that without touching the knife again until the fork is back where it first began and pointing downwards.

It is deeply insulting to the cook if you cut everything into small pieces before eating any of it. Wouldn't you rather be at home, where Mummy could do that for you?

I've seen worse. When I lived in Sydney, a smart young man came to dinner to talk business. I cooked simple food so it would not dominate — steak, baked potatoes, some vegetables. While he tucked in with gusto, I couldn't eat a thing. Before even tasting the food, he not only cut up everything into very small pieces, but he then mixed them together so my careful meal looked like vomit before he'd taken a mouthful. And what a boring mouth his must be — to want every forkful to taste the same. Needless to say we didn't do business — he was planning to run a restaurant!

In countries where British custom prevails, you cut up and eat food without putting down the knife or switching the fork. But don't then peck at your plate like a sun-stunned chook. These peckers have nothing on 'click go the shears, boy'. They click and clatter and peck all over their plate perhaps two dozen times before their fork is loaded, and then, by the time they've unloaded and chewed once, they are clicking and clattering again, knife and fork hitting the plate without cease.

They are breaking a cardinal cutlery rule — the use of cutlery should be as noiseless as the actual eating, otherwise you are attracting attention to yourself and away from the conversation of others. Neither a chopper nor a pecker be. It's mesmerising, but this is not what I want at a table. I could throw crumbs at pigeons.

The cruellest person ever was the one who invented the tortured fork position used by so many Americans when cutting their food. The fork is held upright in the left hand, but with the handle threaded intricately between the fingers in a way I have never been able to replicate. Another common awkwardness is to hold the food down with the knife and to tear at it with the fork. It should be done the other way round.

The cruellest person ever was the one who invented the tortured fork position used by so many Americans when cutting their food.

While you are chewing, your knife and fork should be resting on the plate; but if you are still holding them they should never be pointed upwards. It can be confrontational to others if you use your knife or fork to gesticulate.

When something goes wrong at table, the very worst thing you can do is to draw attention to it or to yourself. It's up to you if you wish to draw attention to someone else's mistakes.

table

26

manners

Setting Standards

Never set just a spoon for the third, sweet course of a meal. We are adults and can therefore do two things at a time, so set a spoon and a fork. Ice cream-style desserts may be served with only a spoon if they come in a long glass, but otherwise it's useful to have a fork to help should the ice cream be too hard to cut with just a spoon.

The spoon and fork for this course are often found set above the table setting, but this is quite wrong in a domestic environment. 'They do it at Buckingham Palace', I hear someone squeak. Well, yes, they do — but they have a thousand people to dinner. Setting a spoon and fork above the plate is for restaurants and banquets. It saves a lot of time to have them there, and, more importantly, it keeps the noise level down. It would be an intrusive and clattery business laying out spoons and forks between courses for a thousand people. It would also take far too long, given all everyone wants is to hear the speeches and then get back to exploring as many of the State Rooms as possible before Carriages and Lights Out.

table

28

manners

When you are entertaining just a few people at home, a spoon and fork above the plate smacks of being anally organised rather than of being hospitable. It suggests a clean and tidy kitchen might be more important to you than what comes out of it.

When you are entertaining just a few people at home, a spoon and fork above the plate smacks of being anally organised rather than being hospitable.

You should always set the pudding spoons and forks closest to the table mat, that is, first in, last out. If you do not have the space for this, lay the setting after clearing the main course. Don't serve the food and then hand them out; this is awkward and draws too much attention to what you are doing.

When you have finished eating a course, your implements should be laid neatly beside each other on the plate, with the fork tines pointing upwards. This is especially important in a restaurant, as it tells the staff you have finished. If you are pausing, or need to leave the table before you have eaten a course, the implements should be crossed in a '20-to-5' position, ideally with the tines pointed down.

If you and your guests are going to be eating informally — inside or outside, from a buffet or barbecue — but will actually sit at a table to eat, it is very bad form to offer cutlery rolled in a napkin. If you have allowed a seat for each guest, then a setting for each should be placed on the table.

When guests are expected to drape themselves against fences, under hydrangeas and precariously on the edge of pots, wrapped cutlery becomes a boon, and as each successive diner drops their knife and fork onto the dog or the ground — or both — many gales of laughter will be heard. Those being laughed at might not accept another invitation. Not always a bad thing, of course.

The Pea Dilemma

I used to think peas had been invented to give us pleasure. Louis XIV certainly thought so and would eat bowls of them without sharing, which I suppose you can get away with if you are the Sun King and it's your Versailles. Now I know peas to be the ultimate table test.

Properly, peas should be crushed onto the fork — a fork with the tines pointing down. The best way is first to have loaded the fork with something to which they will stick, such as potato or a soft vegetable that squashes easily onto the fork. It's sometimes easier to put down your knife and then switch your fork to the other hand, so you can shovel the peas against something else on the plate, thus ensuring that they end up on your fork.

> Properly, peas should be crushed onto the fork – a fork with the tines pointing down.

Unless you are out somewhere really elegant or important, such as dinner with your potential in-laws, or out on a first date, or interviewing household staff (the ones who most cling to 'backstairs refained'), you can get away with using your knife to push peas onto your turned-up fork. Yes, it is the wrong way to use a fork, but with peas this method seems increasingly accepted.

For myself, I never order or accept peas if I am somewhere where I don't feel comfortable, and I only serve them at the most informal meals.

—

table

33

manners

The Nitty Grotty

Here it is — a roll call of some of the most important things to do or not to do at table. Laugh at some if you will, but each of the following rules is based on two simple default positions: (1) do nothing that draws attention to you; and (2) do nothing that invades another diner's comfort zone.

Never, ever, cut a bread roll (or scone or croissant) with a knife, because it is likely to turn to a grey, greasy paste — worse when you squash on butter — and you will look like a country klutz. Pull bread rolls apart, and then break them and put butter only on the part you are eating. This means you do not spread butter on half a roll and then stuff yourself with that. The more you bite off the more you have to chew, and the less you will be able to say. At least, I hope so.

> Pull bread rolls apart, and then break them and put butter only on the part you are eating.

Don't even think of talking when food is in your mouth. You know how to eat, don't you? You close your lips and then chew. Lauren Bacall couldn't have whistled up a better definition.

Don't even think of talking when food is in your mouth.

The gracious and formal way to get butter to bread when you are at the table is to take some butter with the butter knife, put that butter on the side of your plate, and then use your bread-and-butter knife to spread it onto small pieces of bread or roll. The knife that cuts into the butter should never be the one that spreads the butter.

Informally, do what you like, but it's always bad form to reach with your bread-and-butter knife when a butter knife is provided — and worse if in so doing you leave the butter with souvenirs of whatever else you are eating.

There's one thing everyone knows about table manners but nearly everyone chooses to ignore: do not put salt and pepper onto your food until you have tasted it. Spraying salt and pepper over untasted food cooked by someone else is the ultimate arrogance. It displays a belief that, however the food tastes, only you know how to make it edible.

There's one thing everyone knows about table manners but nearly everyone chooses to ignore: do not put salt and pepper onto your food until you have tasted it.

It's common to see fingers going into salt dishes, but it's no more correct than it ever was (see page 10). It's too easy to mark the salt with whatever is on your fingers. The proper way to give yourself salt from an open dish — classically called just a salt, rather than a salt cellar — is to dip in the end of a knife and then to pour that salt in a neat pile onto the side of your plate. This way you can flavour each mouthful individually. If you are offered a salt grinder, you should grind a neat pile on the side of your plate rather than grinding salt all over the food.

Pepper may be ground over food, but if ready-ground pepper is served in a small bowl it, too, should be piled onto the side of your plate.

If the salt or pepper is not directly in front of you, don't stretch to get it. Avoid situations in which your arm has to do anything at an angle because you will be invading someone else's space. Even if the salt and pepper are in front of the person next to you, ask them to pass them.

> If the salt or pepper is not directly in front of you, don't stretch to get it.

When someone asks you to pass the salt, always send the pepper with it, and in doing so do not pass too far in front of anyone else and never pass anything so far you have to rise in your seat. A good fellow guest is always aware of what's happening at the table and will be a relay station without being asked, and so should you.

The same goes for bread or vegetables, mustard or sauces; if they are not directly in front of you, then you must ask for them to be passed. And if you are asked to pass, pass them via other diners rather then leaning over another guest.

Eating soup is a major challenge on the path to social and corporate success. Either the modern rounded soup spoon or the larger traditional one, now more commonly called a tablespoon, can be used. Both spoons can be sipped from the front or the side, but neither goes into the mouth, the way a fork might.

> Eating soup is a major challenge on the path to social and corporate success.

The really important thing is to move the spoon in the soup away from you, from the nearest edge to the furthest edge of the bowl or plate; you do not scoop towards, you but away from you. There is excellent sense behind this, as there is behind each tenet of manners. You then have to pass the spoon back over the bowl and, if it is dripping, the drips will land in the soup and not on you. When it is time to collect the last spoonfuls, you tip the soup plate away from you for the same reasons.

Sit up straight and take food to your mouth and not your mouth to the food. Don't slouch and don't bend your head down to meet the fork halfway. If you must have your mouth close to the food, eat noodles, but somewhere else, please. The poor fellow on the cover is actually doing three things to upset film star David Niven: he's leaning over the table, he's blowing on his food and he has his napkin tied around his neck.

> Sit up straight and take food to your mouth and not your mouth to the food.

Be confident that forks are designed to get all the way to a mouth that's at right angles to an upright neck. So, your food falls everywhere? You put too much on the fork.

Whether small or large, the portion in your mouth should never be seen by others. The amount you put on your fork should never fill even half your mouth. If others can see your cheeks pouched with food, it conjures pictures of what is happening behind those cheeks and that's disturbing.

You should be able to put a fork with food on it into your mouth without a three-point turn. If you truly find it comforting, you may, of course, stuff your mouth and reach humanoid chipmunk status, but not when you are eating in company.

> You should be able to put a fork with food on it into your mouth without a three-point turn.

Neither should food be heard. The noisiest eaters are those who not only chew with an open mouth, but who also churn, using their tongue to turn and twist food, lapping food off their palate onto their bottom teeth, noisily. This is intolerably offensive and totally self-centred. One wonders if they do anything but think of themselves while they masticate. If you aren't too sure about your masticatory habits, try eating a meal in front of a mirror or ask someone to be frank with you.

The speed at which you eat should be matched to that of the other diners. If you are served in the style once called 'dog's dinner', that is with everything already served on your plate, it can be an attractive idea to bog in at once. Indeed there are American books that say this is acceptable. I'm not so sure. It makes you look greedy and thoughtless. Anyway, what if it is a household that says grace before eating?

Unless you are host or hostess, it's always better not to be first to eat, which also means not being the first one to pick up your knife and fork. If you do, and you are wrong, you are marked.

table

45

manners

At a restaurant you should always wait until everyone has been served. If you are invited to begin before that time, do so, but discreetly. In fact a good host will usually invite people to begin before he or she is served. It's not necessary to add the hoary 'while it is hot'. Only the first few mouthfuls are ever truly hot; we tend to eat lukewarm food and thank goodness for that. It tastes much better than piping hot food.

At a restaurant you should always wait until everyone has been served.

Don't leave lip marks on a glass, and I don't mean just lipstick. Whether you're male or female always wipe your lips before drinking, especially if your meal includes anything greasy, oily or fatty, as most do. Grubby smears on glasses are not a pretty sight; it's as bad as seeing teeth jammed with rotting food.

Good conversation is the best seasoner at table, and you should always make a contribution — gruff grunts and a sour expression are a guarantee of permanent unpopularity. At a big table, the norm was for a man first to speak to the woman on his right, to switch to the woman on his left once the main course was served, and then generalise when that was over. Women did the opposite, of course. It remains a good plan.

At a small table, the host or hostess should ensure everyone is included; easy enough if you remember the basic tenet of making conversation, which is never to ask a question that can be answered with 'yes' or 'no'. 'What part of Sweden did you like best?' rather than 'Did you like Sweden?'

At a business lunch or dinner, guests can be mixed in whatever way is served best by its purpose, so long as no one feels left out. It's considered good manners to wait until the main course is served before discussing business.

It's considered good manners to wait until the main course is served before discussing business.

And how might you discover the way someone eats before facing them over a table? Watch how they chew gum. Frankly, gum-chewers are probably a bad bet anyway, but at least it gives a clue. Those who chew gum with their mouth open, sounding like small cows trying to escape deep swamps, are bound to eat the same way. Look somewhere else for a partner, employee or employer.

Putting in a Word

Showing your origins by how you spoke was once something it was better to hide by changing your accent. But too many got rid of their regional or colonial accents without knowing there was more to perceived social position than how one spoke. The words you used also gave you away.

Before the First World War only the very rich could travel, and their international passage was eased by speaking French; although outrageously snobby, it was acceptable to drop a few French words into conversation to indicate your social standing. These were late nineteenth-century times, when so many adventurous farming and labouring men, and women who'd worked in private service, left Europe for new countries, some as far away as New Zealand and Australia. There, they found equality, which was the last thing most of them wanted. Those determined to be thought superior aped their 'betters' at Home by using French words in their new country.

After the First World War, when anyone could travel, the upper classes shuddered; for anyone could now also learn and speak French, and some did. The British higher class, at least, quickly dropped everything French about their speech and subsequently

table
50
manners

the use of French words in conversation became a sure sign of pretension. But not in the countries where British immigrants had settled — there French was still thought a good thing. This may be the case still in your home town, but when you want to move — or work — in top European or American circles, it is as well to know that any word with a French background is probably less acceptable than an English one, except in France. There, they actually have laws against using English and American words like 'sandwich' and 'weekend'.

A list of those words most liable to determine your origins was made famous in an essay by Nancy Mitford in a small book called *Noblesse Oblige*, in which she called them 'U' and 'Non-U' words. Some usages have changed; almost no one says 'looking-glass' any more when they mean 'mirror', or 'over mantel' instead of 'mantelpiece'.

A few of these words are associated with food and entertaining, or being entertained. If you are travelling from Europe to Australia and New Zealand, be prepared to find the very reverse of what you expect to be thought acceptable because French-based words are often preferred in the Southern Hemisphere. Don't, however, allow your defences to crumble and start saying 'toilet'.

> Don't, however, allow your defences to crumble and start saying 'toilet'.

Let's no longer call these 'U' and 'Non-U' words. If we instead allocate them geographically, it will be easier for you to decide if any are important enough to change your vocabulary. Judgements are most made by the use of the following:

UK and Europe	Australasia
lavatory, loo	*toilet*
cake	*gâteau/torte*
sofa	*couch/lounge (Aus)**
drawing/sitting room	*lounge/lounge room (Aus)**
napkin	*serviette*
false teeth	*dentures*

* The curious Australian neologism of calling a sofa a lounge has not been explained but at least makes some sense of having a lounge room in which to put one. In most of the Northern Hemisphere it's as well to remember a lounge is found only in a public building, at an airport or on a ship. Sitting room is always a better term to use than drawing room, unless the latter is unbelievably big.

In both Europe and Australasia, you can also be tripped up on the names you give particular meals, which might not worry you from the manners/etiquette point of view, but it can certainly play havoc with your stomach's expectations of comfort.

table 53 manners

For centuries, dinner was the main meal of the day, once served as early at 10 am and slowly moving later and later, until by the late eighteenth century it was often served at 4 pm. Then it got even later and became an evening meal, served as late as 10 pm. At least it did if you were an aristocrat or one of the emerging middle class, with an office.

For the ordinary working man, dinner never got past what he ate in the middle of the day, even if it were just a sandwich. In the evening he and his family ate supper. And then along came tea, the first hot drink the poor ever had.

The working man then had a meal called tea when he came home, sometimes the most substantial meal of the day but still followed up by supper before he went to bed, so there was never very long between meals for him. Pity the aristocrats in their great houses with nothing to eat between the newly invented meal of lunch and a very late dinner.

Tea was drunk in such houses at any time of the day, but a hot drink wasn't enough for Sarah, eighth Duchess of Bedford, who found it difficult to stay conscious until dinner-time. In the middle of the afternoon she would ask for tea and something substantial to eat with it, which was served in her boudoir (private sitting room), rather than in the drawing room, thus establishing from the start this was a meal based on intimacy and lack of public pretence or show. It was called tea. The afternoon was taken for granted, just as she and her kind only go riding, and never horse-riding.

Once lesser levels of society caught onto the idea of tea, it raised a problem — they already had a meal called tea. So they called the new one afternoon tea, indicating there'd be another one later.

The way it works today is like this. People who have dinner in the middle of the day then serve afternoon tea followed by tea; people who have lunch will serve tea in the afternoon and then dinner at night. It is important to get this right when you change hemispheres. I found it very distressing to be asked if I wanted an egg or some biscuits for tea, when I still expected tea to be my main evening meal. If you aren't sure, ask.

An authentic tea/afternoon tea served in the afternoon should be simple: a straightforward cake, perhaps a chocolate cake or a fruit cake, sandwiches that are dainty but well flavoured, and something hot such as toast, scones, tea cakes, crumpets, etc. This light, afternoon meal is never eaten at a table.

In the north of England you might be asked to choose a fancy, a cream cake perhaps, but elsewhere cream cakes and pastries are properly the domain of cafés and tea shops rather than the home.

High tea is something else again, a light meal eaten at a table in the late afternoon and which must also offer a savoury hot dish — anything from grilled sardines on toast to a hot meat pie, which is also usually a hint you should fill up and not expect much for supper that night. If there is nothing hot, it is not high tea.

table 56 manners

Throughout the world, hotel staff think high tea is anything with cream cakes and a high price, but this is a cream tea rather than the light meal the name properly indicates.

> Throughout the world, hotel staff think high tea is anything with cream cakes and a high price...

It is very lowering of hotels to get it so wrong, and continuing proof that two-week groundings in IT do absolutely nothing to improve an employee's background in international etiquette and manners. Why, one even sees hotel staff members who do up the bottom button of their waistcoats.

table
57
manners

Completely vexing for everyone is the use of the word 'entrée'. In the Northern Hemisphere, an entrée is the main course; this is a left-over from gargantuan Victorian and Edwardian menus in which a 'made-up' dish of something with a sauce preceded, or was an entrée to, the roast. The roast as a separate course has disappeared altogether and may now even be your entrée.

In Australia and New Zealand, the fixation on the idea that anything French must be better if it has something to do with food means entrée is used to mean first course. Oh, the confusion this causes to foreign visitors!

Wherever you come from or go to, it is easier on everyone if you speak only of first and main courses. That way you'll never be wrong and affect your entrée into Society.

Students of solecism can do no better than to learn by heart John Betjeman's poem 'How to Get On in Society', which begins with the immortal lines:

'Phone for the fish knives, Norman,
Cook's feeling terribly unnerved . . .

Scents and Sensibilities

Don't smell. It's as simple as that. Very few people today think it smart to advertise their intimate scents. The exceptions — those who think it clever not to wear deodorant — don't realise how intrusive they are because they rarely smell themselves: noses are brilliant at cutting off constant smells with which they are bored. Even if you smell terrible, you might not think so, because your nose is protecting you from it by ignoring it.

Musky Earth Mother and sweaty Earth Father are not good concepts where food is being served and can nauseate others, however much these same stinks stimulate your regular Friday night callers. Napoleon famously wrote to Josephine saying he would be home the next night: 'Don't wash,' he added, but they were unlikely to be going out to eat.

table 60 manners

Smelling of anything too much is very bad manners at table. It is about as wrong as it's possible to be to turn up at a meal in billows of scent, after-shave, or cologne or smelling too strongly of an expensive soap, shampoo or, particularly, deodorant. Cheap ones are infinitely worse.

> It is about as wrong as it's possible to be to turn up at a meal in billows of scent, after-shave, or cologne . . .

Many men seem to go for smelly deodorants, quite unaware they are boorishly replacing one confrontational smell with another. Scentless/perfume-free deodorants work as well — and more acceptably.

The senses of smell and scent are pretty much the same thing, and if you are overpowering others with the rip-off you bought on a Hong Kong side-street you are preventing them from enjoying their meal. You should have known anyway and stopped yourself, because wearing too much scent is just another way of attracting attention, and we don't do this at table, whether at home or being entertained.

You should only be aware of how expensive — or how rottenly chemical — a man or woman may smell when you are near enough to kiss them. The trick, by the way, is to apply the scent you prefer only to areas covered by clothes; the chest is perhaps best, although there was a famously fascinating French aristocrat who revealed the secret of her bewitching enchantment was to wear scent only below her waist. This works well for men and for women, but not too far below the waist. Save that for evenings likely to end with your being invited to fold your table napkin (see page 92).

Provided you do it discreetly, it is not bad manners to ask someone to leave a table and to wash off an intrusive scent. If the problem is that they or their clothes actually need a wash, I should remember another engagement as far away as possible.

Yes, even if it is a job interview I have to leave. No one who smells too much at table can be trusted to tell you the truth about your prospects, social or corporate.

If it is you who is the stinker, don't be surprised if you don't get the call.

Raw onions should never be eaten if you are going on to business or social intercourse. You can't smell it, but your breath reeks of raw onion for hours and it is horrid for others. If you do eat raw onion at lunch or dinner (why would you?), clean your teeth and your tongue afterwards. Chewing gum does not do it.

> Raw onions should never be eaten if you are going on to business or social intercourse.

In spite of what they say in TV commercials, it's not germs that cause bad breath, and bad digestion usually goes the other way. It's more likely to be rotting food wedged between your teeth, and knowing this you'll want to be super careful about mouth hygiene. Ideally, this is not something done at table.

Please do not suck your teeth free of debris when others are around, and don't pick at them with fingernails — your teeth that is, not the others.

Toothpicks are used at table only if you are in a state of great distress, and you should hold one hand over your mouth while picking with the other. Just as it is polite to not be the first to start eating, it's best not to be first to use a toothpick. But if you must, just get on with doing it and neither apologise nor make any other comment.

If you expect dinner to lead to breakfast, carry dental floss.

In the Restaurant

Here's where you must remember everything Nanny ever taught you, even if you never had a nanny. Restaurants are as much theatres of life as places to go when you are hungry. How you conduct yourself is likely to be an audition for the rest of your life, and more romances, friendships and job opportunities are lost in restaurants than in any other place.

And it's not just your own reputation to consider. You are as likely to be judged by the behaviour and manners of whoever you are dining with, too.

Start by getting there on time; if you can't, telephone your companion/s or call the restaurant and ask them to pass your message on. Contradictory as it might seem, good manners are what mobile phones do best.

Contradictory as it might seem, good manners are what mobile phones do best.

Computers, telephones, pagers and the like have no place in a restaurant — just how important do you think you are? If you are expecting something major to happen, leave your telephone at the reception desk, asking them to answer it and to take a message or to come and get you. A handsome reward is in order.

If you are eating from a buffet, ignore what others might do and do not pile your plate with several layers of food. Nothing is more sickening to see. Make a nice plateful, eat it and then go back for more. Surely you don't want to look as though it's the first time you have eaten for a week? How sad does that make your personal life look?

If you have to order from a menu, do not read the entire dish description. If the menu offers *Icelandic cod cheeks with puffballs of lentilles de Puy, aged tangerine peel, over-wrought potatoes and a jus of Arbroath smokies*, then simply tell the waiter you want the fish. If there is more than one fish on the menu, ask for the cod.

It's only necessary to order your first two courses because: (a) the waiter couldn't be less interested in your sweet tooth at this stage; and (b) at a business lunch or an out-of-town dinner venue, time might not allow a third course.

Feel no shame about asking if a dish has an ingredient you don't like, but rather than making a fuss and demanding the vegetarian pasta without the vegetables but with a rare steak, order something you know you will like.

Please don't make a conversational thing of it with the waiter or waitress; they are there to feed only your culinary appetites.

Please don't make a conversational thing of it with the waiter or waitress; they are there to feed only your culinary appetites.

Food allergies, which can be food malabsorption problems, but in my experience are more likely to be a fad or a fashion, should be revealed to a host or hostess before accepting an invitation. If you are the one with the problem, mention it at the time you are invited to someone's house or have a quick chat to the restaurant beforehand to make sure they can cope.

Although it seems unbelievable, there are some people who are prepared to arrive at a lunch or dinner and only then announce they are Sino-Tibetan vego-lactarians, or they can eat black pepper only if it's been white pepper, or they find it impossible to sit at a table with anyone who breathes at more than the average rate.

They are the ones most likely to ask for ice cubes to go in the Châteauneuf-du-Pape and then exclaim they had forgotten they are 'allergic' to tannin, glass, alcohol, cold and the colour red. Don't be one of them. Don't entertain one.

If someone does this to you, show them the bread, a knife and the refrigerator. Actually, forget the bread and the refrigerator.

If someone does this to you, show them the bread, a knife and the refrigerator. Actually, forget the bread and the refrigerator.

If you are hosting at a restaurant, it's a neat and much respected thing for you to collect everyone's order and then to give these to the waiter on your guests' behalf. It reinforces your place in the pecking order, shows the staff you have eaten out before, and to whom they should be particularly nice if they want a tip. Be sure you can do it without making notes on your cuff, or don't do it at all.

Ask your waiter or waitress (no one with class knows what a waitperson is) if you should order everyone's first course and then everyone's main, or if you should give the first and main courses guest by guest.

It's very impressive if you mention your guests by name: 'Mr Stewart will have the caviar and salmon, Miss Stewart will have the pâté and salmon, Miss David will have steak tartare, but only a very little onion, followed by the turbot, and I'll have the caviar and the salmon.' Don't forget what you are doing and let it slip Miss David would actually prefer to have Mr Stewart followed by Miss Stewart, and is open to other configurations.

table
71
manners

Once the food has been ordered there is no reason for you to have any further interaction with the staff. You do not need to thank them for putting the food in front of you, but a brief, quiet polite acknowledgement of your gratitude is appreciated when they do. The same goes for staff in houses.

This concept of essentially ignoring staff might be baffling to those who live in Australia and New Zealand, where your order tends to be sought by someone who crouches or kneels beside you. A feisty and notably aged woman from Europe once asked the gorgeous young man at her knee if there was something else he was expecting to do for her while down there. He was very soon upright, but in the nice way.

●

Wine Bluffs

If you are the one choosing the wine, don't dither and don't show off. If you know nothing about wine, put on a smile and say, 'Why don't we begin with the house white/red/sparkling/champagne?'

That then gives time for someone who knows more to think about a better bottle to follow. Don't play dumb and ask the sommelier to make a suggestion; he or she is trained to recommend something more expensive than had you first considered and you won't want to look cheap by refusing it. But if you do end up in this situation, simply reply, 'Mmm, I've never really enjoyed that.'

Those who do know about wine should not lecture on the merits or demerits of the wine list, and shouldn't weigh the possibilities of each bottle individually. The best bet is to look for something unusual you know and can say a couple of words about.

As for food and wine matching, the old rules of red with red meat and white with white meat and fish are well gone. Sometimes a white wine can be heavier than a red, while a red can be lighter than a white. These days matching is more usually done by weight: a lightweight red or white wine for light food; a heavyweight red or white for heavy food.

> These days matching is more usually done by weight: a lightweight red or white wine for light food; a heavyweight red or white for heavy food.

If all this is still over your head, you might care to know that more and more people now appreciate the herbal freshness of a well-made, dry rosé wine, particularly as a combined aperitif and first-course wine.

table 75 manners

Ask the waiter which is the driest rosé if you suspect some might be off-dry or sweetish. The rosé will be a good talking point and, of course, tends to go with whatever has been ordered as a first course. You've been special without being a snob or talking down to the others.

—

table
76
manners

Hot Stuff

A meal in an Asian or Oriental restaurant is no reason to think manners aren't needed. There are right and wrong ways to handle yourself and your implements, at least there are if you do not want to be misjudged.

Thai restaurants set the table with a spoon and fork, and most Westerners eat with the fork. This is considered rather common by Thais, who always eat with the spoon, as should you.

A properly ordered Thai meal is based on each dish being cooked a different way — one steamed, one poached, one deep-fried, one stir-fried and so on. It is profoundly bad manners to put a serving of more than one dish at a time onto the rice, thus mixing up the carefully different flavours and textures. Equally, it

It is profoundly bad manners to put a serving of more than one dish at a time onto the rice, thus mixing up the carefully different flavours and textures.

is very rude to pile too much of a favourite dish onto your rice before others have had their share.

Soup is not a first course, but should be sipped as a palate freshener throughout the meal.

In Thai and Indian restaurants you are likely to be confronted by food that is very chilli-hot. Chilli is not a flavour but an agent of pain, and it's the way chilli burns the tongue that gives you a good feeling; the brain manufactures serotonins to give you a high in return for the pain you have suffered. This has nothing whatsoever to do with good food, and chilli has long been used by the very poor in areas of Asia so they get some sense of pleasure out of a miserable bowl of rice and scraps of vegetable.

The constantly scarred tongue of those who have eaten chilli since childhood means they are largely inured to the heat and, even though a dish might taste hot to you or me, it is barely 'warm' to their palate. To avoid the worst excesses of hot food, say in Indian and Thai restaurants, you should also eat the traditional way, too. Whether eating with a spoon or fork, you should always have as much rice as curry in each mouthful so the chilli is diluted; this is of course what happens when an Asian or Oriental eats with their hands.

No Indian or Thai diner would ever have a mouthful of just curry or a similar dish; they will also eat rice at the same time.

No Indian or Thai diner would ever have a mouthful of just curry or a similar dish; they will also eat rice at the same time.

The best thing to soothe a burned palate is yoghurt or something else fatty with a dairy base, like butter or cheese. Milk can help, but the very worst thing you can do is to drink water, beer or anything carbonated. It's the oil in the chilli that's burning you and these liquids don't dissolve it but run off it, often spreading the oil as they go.

Most people who suffer from an upset stomach after an Indian or Thai meal blame the chilli. It's true, but the chilli only became a problem because it was eaten with too much liquid, causing the ground chilli to be flushed out of the stomach onto the intestine walls. If little or no liquid was taken, other than yoghurts, fruit, pickles etc, the chilli would have passed through the system still mixed with the other ingredients and would have caused far fewer problems. Yes, even beer is best left for other times.

Chinese restaurants seem cooler about mixing several dishes together on your rice, but it's still not the way to get the best meal. More important to remember is not to reach for food from a dish with your chopsticks, but to spoon or slide it onto your rice — just as you would not use a fork you have eaten from to serve yourself from a dish at home. Many restaurants also put a set or two of longer chopsticks on the table and these should be specifically reserved for serving.

Chopstick etiquette dictates that you should never stick chopsticks upright in a dish and leave them like that, as this is a reminder of memorials to the dead.

table
82
manners

You are allowed to be noisier than normal when eating such meals, but only in the right place; chopsticks or spoons are not an invitation to eat noisily. The dispensation comes only when eating noodles, but within reason, which is why it's acceptable to hold the bowl very close to your mouth — as you can also do with rice.

You are allowed to be noisier than normal when eating such meals, but only in the right place; chopsticks or spoons are not an invitation to eat noisily.

The slurping that's acceptable when sucking up noodles, whether in Korea, Japan, China, Birmingham or Wellington, is based on deep-seated Oriental symbolism; noodles represent longevity and so to bite or break them is to put your future at risk. You see? There is always a reason for what's thought good manners and what's not.

The Folding Stuff

We've all seen them — the ones who don't know what to do with their table napkin when they finish eating. They secretly envy the neatness of those who forcefully fold theirs back into the original creases. They openly admire the wilfulness of those who simply fling and fly. In the end they equivocate by folding untidily. Someone always notices.

Both folding and crumpling of one's napkin are right, but at different times.

Good manners dictate you fold a table napkin when you are staying for more than one meal or overnight in someone else's house. It signals you are happy to use it again, that your host or hostess is not expected to wash and iron overnight, and you don't arrogantly expect them to have piles in the linen cupboard just to gratify your elevated sensitivities.

table

86

manners

Both folding and crumpling of one's
napkin are right, but at different times.

This is when napkin rings are properly used, and it saves a lot of confusion if these are set on the table. You then fold and roll the napkin neatly in its ring when the meal is over; it can be left at the place setting or, if each napkin ring is easily identifiable, can be put away until the next meal. It is pretentious to set napkin rings for guests who will eat and then leave.

At all other times you should leave your napkin crumpled. Crumpling your napkin is the rule in restaurants, cafés, hotels, cruise ships and aircraft. No matter which class you are travelling, there will be clean napkins next time you eat. Some older boarding houses and B&B establishments might not run to clean napkins every meal so you will get your own back, in the napkin ring they will have provided.

table
87
manners

Leaving a napkin folded when it should be crumpled signals social naïveté in the young; in anyone with a job it shows obstinate inability to observe and learn from what goes on around you, or that you are a compulsive neatnik, rarely a compliment.

These days, if just two of you have been dining privately, leaving a folded napkin on the dinner table might be interpreted as a willingness to stay for breakfast.

There is nothing wrong with paper napkins, as long as they are at least three-ply, very absorbent and very big. Thinner ones are usually meanly sized too, useless for anything but blowing your nose. Gently, even then.

table 88 manners

These days, if just two of you have been dining privately, leaving a folded napkin on the dinner table might be interpreted as a willingness to stay for breakfast.

I try to avoid eating in restaurants that use small, thin paper napkins. They might have a wonderful chef, but management knows nothing about eating. As for finding these miserable things in other people's houses, well, it makes me wonder if they can afford to have me there at all.

Like damask, linen or cotton, white is the best colour for paper napkins. Otherwise you might be confused with those who still throw themed dinners or, worse, to be drawing attention to your new carpet by picking up the rose-purple tones of the blowsier swirls with the magenta napkins. Next thing you know, you'll be taking napkin-folding lessons.

Folding napkins into fans, swans or starbursts belongs only to fancy restaurants and to the very grandest dinner parties at the very grandest of mansions. Even at such restaurants and dinners, nothing is smarter to look at, easier to unravel, or gives more encouragement about what is to follow than nicely starched, simply folded white damask, linen or cotton table napkins. Cloth napkins or three-ply paper ones can be coloured at lunch-time to indicate informality, and I suppose would do if you are dining in the kitchen or in bed. Yet nothing quite matches the delicious wantonness of unfolding a starchy white napkin to eat baked beans on toast.

table 90 manners

Bread is never served at formal dinners, and so the napkin should go in the middle of each person's table setting. Never, ever, in the wine glasses. That is what window dressers do at work.

At lunch, the napkin can be placed on the bread-and-butter plate. Bread is never served at formal dinners, and so the napkin should go in the middle of each person's table setting. Never, ever, in the wine glasses. That is what window dressers do at work.

Whatever the prices in a restaurant, there is likely to be someone swishing about to unfold and then slither your napkin across your lap. Give in, if this is unavoidable. Otherwise it is perfectly correct to do it yourself, and the sooner the better because it saves embarrassment and gets you a drink faster. In smart restaurants, the napkin swisher won't be saying much, and so this casts an awkward pall over the table until everyone has been done. In casual restaurants, the swisher sneakily uses this time to start their wearisome 'waitperson' patter. The faster you get napkins onto your lap, the sooner both types have to get on with their real job. A savvy host or hostess cuts them short by firmly ordering drinks.

In a private house you should unfold your table napkin as soon as you sit down. It's a commonly understood symbol you are engaged with the table, ready to talk and to be talked to, to sing for your lunch or supper. Do a good job and you might be invited to fold your napkin later.

Unless you are obese and have no choice, it is gross to tuck a napkin into your collar. It's the sort of thing hearty students think the sign of a jolly trencherman; but you don't have to be at university to work out that eating greedily shouldn't mean dribbling food down your front.

Unless you are obese and have no choice, it is gross to tuck a napkin into your collar.

And that leaves table napkin etiquette for nudists:

- stand to eat
- lean well forward
- some women might find it useful to fling an arm across their chest.

Dressing
the Balance

If you are not very experienced in big city ways, and need to make a good impression, there are several things to get right, especially in restaurants.

Although hovering on the very edge of acceptability in Australasia, it is considered very bad manners in most other countries for a man to remove his jacket and hang it over the back of his chair before sitting down.

In London, for instance, you would seem out of touch with where you are, and that's not useful. If you are not certain, leave your jacket on until you can see the way others are coping. You might have to get used to dining in your jacket.

In most European cities it is still common for men to dine in coats and ties whilst women are cool in strapless frocks. If the heat is unbearable, the host is the one who should suggest that gentlemen might remove their jackets. Sneer at this if you like, but if you want that man or that woman or that job, you'll do it their way.

table
94
manners

Drinks before a meal are another occasion not to be different. Beer might be your choice, but look around. Unless it's lunchtime, and you are in a café, and it's very bright and sunny, a glass of beer before lunch can look very rural. Anyway, with that much liquid sloshing around, where will lunch go?

Certainly, personal style might mean you get away with it, but ordering a glass of beer as an aperitif — plus hanging your jacket over the back of your chair — will surely mark you as a hick or a colonial. In some cases this will be a good thing, but only if you get what you want. On a practical note, a jacket on the back of a chair is also an easy target for pick-pockets, and if you take off your jacket it's always a good idea to keep your wallet about you.

Once stultifying, dress rules are becoming much more casual in the United Kingdom and Continental Europe with very few but the grandest hotels and restaurants demanding that men wear a tie. It's become super smart for men to wear a very good suit with very, very good shoes and a very, very, very good shirt with French cuffs and cufflinks — but no tie. Telephone the restaurant and ask if you are not sure.

In such grand European restaurants, the pale suits so robustly donned by men throughout Australasia are sometimes not considered suitable, not even at lunch-time, and I have seen people dressed in these asked to leave; once it was my guest at the Ritz Casino. Corduroy suits are equally unacceptable. A dark blazer is a safer and more acceptable bet.

Shoes are an absolute giveaway. Nothing to do with good manners, you might say, but it shows good manners to respect the accepted etiquette of the people with whom you are dining and where you are dining.

For men, pale-coloured shoes of any hue, and with soft soles, are just too casual for anything other than a casual café. Grey shoes are pathetic whatever time or day or whatever the country; my theory is it's women who choose grey or cream shoes for their men, and that the men who let them do so deserve the sniggers they will get.

In European capitals and in better business circles everywhere, men should not wear brown shoes after 6 pm. Change to black — or wear black shoes all day long.

There are few rules about what women should wear in restaurants, except that jewellery must not be noisy; earrings must not jingle, and bracelets must not jangle. Jewellery might, however, shock with expense or flashy bliiiing — where else would you wear such lavishness?

There are few rules about what women should wear in restaurants, except that jewellery must not be noisy; earrings must not jingle, and bracelets must not jangle.

table 97 manners

Long hair attracts unnecessary attention, and this often seems to be what the wearer wants when she has to hold back a hank to get food into her mouth. She may think it looks cute or sexy or fascinating, but it's actually very suburban, just overt pretension and attention-seeking. Long hair should be permanently held back from the food by something other than hands.

There should be less flesh than frock. Very short skirts and low-cut tops are for teenagers and would-be pop stars. If there are cameras about, such dress draws too much attention, and that's cheap in public. It will not be appreciated by your host or hostess if your flesh gets more attention than the money they are spending on you.

> Very short skirts and low-cut tops are for teenagers and would-be pop stars.

Do not for a second believe it is all so much freer in the United States. California might seem more casual and familiar, but it's not. If you take off your jacket, it is much more likely to be taken from you and hung than being left on the chair.

In the great Eastern cities, in fact almost anywhere on the Eastern Seaboard, restaurants can be far pickier about formality than in Europe; they have grander décor and table settings, still offer menus in French, and insist on extraordinary rules about how you should dress. For example, I turned 50 in New York, on New Year's Day. My friends were taking me to lunch at Windows on the World, at the top of the World Trade Centre. We didn't even get as far as the lift to take us up to the restaurant. On New Year's Day, at lunch-time, in a touristy restaurant, I was expected to wear a tie, and they had none to offer me, as they would at, say, at Browns Hotel or the Connaught in London.

Don't be caught out in the States, but always ask about the standard of dress required. Casual still won't mean you can wear grey shoes with those 'nice'n'ezy' Velcro fasteners. Learn how to tie laces on leather shoes again.

Of course, if you want to be associated with those who live in trailer parks and who eat dinner at 5.30 pm, feel free to slouch in wearing 'trainers'.

Things are far different in cafés and diners and such, where it is all much more casual — other than not eating from your knife, not eating with your mouth open, and cutting rather than pulling and breaking rolls, scones, croissants and the like.

You might also have to think more clearly what sort of coffee you order. When in Europe, you should brace yourself for jaw-dropping disbelief if you order a cappuccino coffee after 10 am. Milk is considered food and not a drink. Milk-based coffees are a breakfast drink, and drunk even then with very little food — a croissant rather than a fry-up.

A large cup of hot milky coffee taken before, with, or after lunch or dinner is considered gross; this includes the flat white or latte. With a cake or biscuit, one of these milky coffees is acceptable in mid-afternoon.

Paying the Price

I t is rotten manners to sit at a restaurant table trying to sort out who has spent what. I once saw four women at Auckland's smart revolving Sky Tower restaurant who actually swept aside everything on the table, tipped out their purses of loose change and counted it into piles; they were terrified, it seemed, of returning to their hometown with a handful of foreign coin and of 'losing on the exchange rate'. There were people waiting for tables well within their line of sight.

This is café/diner behaviour, and even there would be pretty low. Agree in advance which of you will pay and settle up later. Or, if you know in advance that you are going to be splitting the bill, make sure you each have what seems enough cash and then give it to your money prefect before you even enter the restaurant.

Agree in advance which of you will pay and settle up later.

Squabbling over money and who had what in a restaurant rates as highly in the Scraping-Fingernails-on-Blackboard Hall of Fame as washing dishes between courses at home.

The latter breaks the mood, shatters any sense of hospitality, interrupts conversations, and excludes guests so they feel they should not have come. It takes no more time to do dishes after guests have gone. And why is it that those who fill the dishwasher always have dishwashers that are so noisy they would be banned if they had four wheels and indicators?

Anyway, guests have made up their mind about how clean and tidy and organised you are within seconds of arriving.

People who grovel for Good Kitchen Fairy points don't get them.

table

103

manners

Does It Really Matter?

We all know people who break rules and yet are chastised by none. That's because they are otherwise charming, good listeners interested in other people and appropriately dressed. Whatever else they do, they do not smell, do not eat with their mouth open or off their knife. Almost everything else can be forgiven someone who is good to be around.

Never confuse good manners
with good sense.

But never confuse good manners with good sense. It is good sense not to entertain or to be entertained if misery makes you feel so bad you can't make a contribution to a table.

It's equally good sense not to entertain or go out when you are afflicted with something contagious or infectious. You will not be thought noble for being a martyr, but a thoughtless ass for putting other people at risk.

And if you suddenly can't bear the thought of eating with someone, lie convincingly and face-savingly to avoid doing it. Life is too short to be well-mannered to someone you don't admire, but not so short you can get away with being rude to them.

Save their face when you cry off, or invent a sick relative or unexpected visitor. Ideally keep a morsel of truth in your excuse. You need such a good memory to tell absolute lies.

Let's give Oscar Wilde his usual apt last word:

In matters of grave importance, style, not sincerity,
is the vital thing.

Index

t
a
b
l
e

109

m
a
n
n
e
r
s

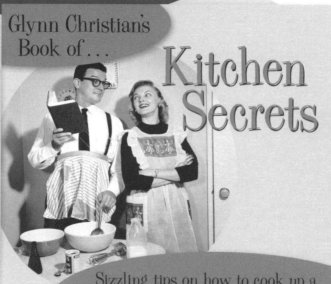

If you enjoyed this book, then look out for...

Glynn Christian's Book of...

Kitchen Secrets

Sizzling tips on how to cook up a dream and achieve success on a plate